The War on Junkies

Freddie Jay

This is a true story, but the names have been changed
to protect the not-so-innocent. All opinions in this book
are those of the author and are not intended as
treatment for addiction or anything else.

Chapters

Foreword

When I finished the book *A Junkie's Nightmare: Coming Clean*, I knew I wanted to continue writing—I just wasn't sure of what I wanted to write about. I have to write about things I know, and that kind of left astrophysics out of it, so I went to what I know best: addiction. I know my way around addiction, and unfortunately, know my way around a prison cell. They kind of go hand in hand. The things I learned along the way, and the things I witnessed, could fill many pages, but I'll stick to the best and the worst for the purposes of this book. I don't plan to speak from my soapbox—I don't have a degree in penology; I'm not a cop, lawyer or affiliated with law enforcement in anyway... wait a minute... That's the speech I give hookers, but nevertheless, I'm none of those things. However, I have spent a great deal of time in police stations, court rooms, jails, prisons, probation and parole offices during my years of active addiction. I'm not exactly proud of this, but it does qualify me as one who has an insider's (pardon the pun) knowledge of our system.

For those of you who didn't read my first book, I'll give you a little background on who I am. I was born in Baltimore, Maryland, in March of a long time ago. My father was a beer-drinking, two-fisted kind of man, short on parenting skills and patience, and he raised me in a house where stolen goods and drunken fights (as well as dope deals and domestic violence) were the norm. My mother was a willing participant in her own misery even before the cancer grabbed her and put her completely at my father's mercy. He sold her pain pills, but made sure she had cheaper substitutes to keep her stoned and docile. Further evidence of their superior childrearing abilities was the fact that I had two older brothers who were doing long prison sentences and a sister who ran away to get married to the first guy who ask her, leaving me at home with a father who was a maniacal tyrant and a mother with stoned indifference .

I started smoking weed and drinking very young; popping pills and snorting cocaine would soon follow—and before 2007, when I finally got clean, I had tried just about everything, but mostly I did heroin and cocaine together in a mixture called speedballs. My oldest brother, John, played a pivotal role in my addiction. I mean, not that I wouldn't have found it anyway, but the condensed version of the story goes like this:

My oldest brother was home after getting paroled from a murder beef down South. He and my father had a history, and the tension between them was always thick, so my father watched him close, but me, not so much. My brother asked me to get him some of the pills my father sold—the pills were Dilaudid, a favorite among junkies because they could be crushed, mixed with water and injected. I told my brother I'd get him some pills if he would show me how to shoot up. He agreed. He never really liked me, and I guess from his point of view, he would be benefitting from something I was bound to do anyway. I loved the opiate high immediately, but it wouldn't really get out of control until that same brother walked in my father's house and put three bullets in my father's head.

Both my brother and my mother were charged with murder and conspiracy and all that (to get that the full story, check out my book *A Junkie's Nightmare: Coming Clean*). I mention that life-changing event here because it's where I went from bad to much worse!! Those choices would lead me to many jails and prisons, many more emergency room visits, a few institutions and damn near death. It's the prison stays I want to focus on a bit. Isn't it funny how those two subjects—addiction and prison—go hand in hand? I dream of a day when addiction is looked at as a social problem and is treated by the medical field instead of being prosecuted in the criminal field. A day when prison is reserved for dangerous criminals and not for people who suffer with a disease. I'm going to let you know right now that I march to the beat of my own drummer and the words in this book are mine, I don't have agendas or political aspirations, just lots of opinions— opinions I intend to share in the following pages about who goes to jail, why they go to jail, what are the core problems and what can we do about it. I don't think I have all the answers, but some answers are looking us directly in the face, and if I can see the glaring inconsistencies, surely others have, too. I mean we elect smart people right? Oh, nevermind. We are the people who voted George W. into office... twice! Of course there are many people who say he's never been elected to anything other than governor, but I digress. I don't know the man or politics, for that matter—he's just easy to make a joke on.

Back to business for a moment, I've been in some very dangerous jails, and I've seen people who just didn't belong in prison, Now, please don't get me wrong, I'm not one of these people who thinks the guy who killed his whole family and three people who look like them is just misunderstood. No, lock his ass up and throw away the key. Prisons were built with those kinds of individuals in mind; at least I think they were. But along the way, our prisons have turned from places of punitive reflection for the morally deficient and criminally minded to multi-million dollar businesses that also house the mentally ill and chemically dependent, so let's take a look at just who occupies our present houses of correction.

My Experience

Before we start with my opinions, how 'bout I tell you about my experience with the criminal "just-us" system? I like to call it the just-us system because the system seems to work in favor of some while it works to destroy others! I'm going to tell you about me, and while I hope to gain readers and sell books, I won't pretty-up who I was or the things I've done. I'll leave it to you as to whether you wish to forgive me or not. I've done things that I live with daily, but that is, as they say, another story.

My first scrape with the law wasn't pleasant. I got locked up with less than a gram of pot at fifteen years old and sent to a task program that's supposed to deter kids from getting involved in the drug culture. My parents left the room and this task officer tore me apart for forty-five minutes verbally. I won't lie—the man never put his hands on me, but some things hurt much worse than a smack to the face. He called me names, said I'd die a junkie; he even talked about the way I dressed. I don't know if this was part of the task program or if I got a guy who just didn't like me, but if that man is still alive, I'd love to spit in his eye. I walked out of there feeling more rebellious than ever. I needed someone to hear me, to reach out to me, but this guy emptied all his anger and frustration on me and I carried his words for many years! "You're nothin' but a junkie!"

It was the '80s and everyone was getting tough on crime. People were fed up. The drugs wars were going on in Florida and cocaine was flooding the streets—and with it came lots of money and blood. The cocaine influx was running right up I-95 and into our back yards. Americans couldn't get enough of it, and the cartels were fighting for dollars, even though there was plenty of money to go around. And that's because there's another thing that comes with cocaine, blood and dollars: greed. It was a ripe time for some people who couldn't handle power to become powerful overnight. Reagan was two years into his presidency and his administration not only set the stage for today's economic struggles, but when it came to addiction, he set us ten years behind the rest of the world. But more on the Reagan administration later.

Anyway, that was the setting in the '80s, and I would get swept up in the get tough on drugs and tougher sentencing laws, along with a lot of other sick people. I think it's worth noting that I'm absolutely convinced that addiction is a disease and that quitting takes much more than will power or just saying, "No!" Drugs change brain function in ways that compulsion takes over and the addict can't quit, in spite of the glaring fact that it is destroying him physically, mentally and spiritually. Yes, maybe in the beginning a person takes drugs of his own free will, but even then, it's more than likely that said individual is hiding from something, covering up something or, at the very least, not wanting to face life on life's terms. But once the drug takes hold and the compulsion is more than you can bear, you have given over any free will you have and will do nearly anything to get the drug. All choices are gone, and you become a victim of your compulsion.

The difference between this disease and other diseases is the damage it inflicts on others. Health issues and crime cost in the neighborhood of $650 billion a year and are in direct relation to drug abuse. That figure doesn't include lost wages or the damage done to the family that can't be measured in dollars and cents. The addict burns bridges with mothers, fathers and anyone who loves them in pursuit of his drug of choice. Please understand that we don't choose this—it chooses us, and we are at its mercy.

Without help, our compulsions lead us to jail, institutions and death, and we are simply passengers along for the ride that we hate. I have actually cried while shooting heroin because I hated myself so much, but was powerless to stop. I hope this book changes minds about addicts—we aren't weak or morally depraved, and we can't stop because we love you. We suffer from an insidious disease that is fatal if left unchecked. Please continue to read this book to understand the nature of addiction from an addict who's been there and back. And if you're an addict, please continue to read this book to understand your actions and to understand the War on Junkies!

What Happened to Freddie Jay?

You may find it hard to believe that I was a shy, quiet kid with puppy-dog eyes who loved his mother dearly, but it's all true. I was a likable kid, but after I started dabbling in drugs, well, trouble would soon follow:'

My criminal career started early, but before I hit the big time, I was locked up with a boatload of pills and a gun. I was sent to The Maryland Training School for Boys. It was there I would get my education in all things criminal. In very short order, I made my mark as one of the tough guys—within twelve hours I picked a fight over a seat and showed the fellas I was not to be disrespected. I felt so clever at the time—and looking back, it was the right move from a survival standpoint—but it was a precursor of things to come. There were two shot callers on the section, one white and one black. I was taking the white spot and everyone knew it. The white shot caller was a tough South Baltimore boy everyone called Reds; the black shot caller was a guy I gave the nickname Marked Money. I think his first name was Mark, and this kid was into any hustle that would turn a dollar. So you can see where I came up with the nickname. Anyway I had a problem with Reds because everyone liked him, and if they all backed him, my coup could be short-lived. As it just so happened, I was at court being committed to training school on the same day Reds had a court appearance. It was there that I found out that he was charged with a sex crime against his little sister.

Reds told everybody he had drug dealing and gun charges, which was actually what I had. So here's prison politics in a nutshell, I had charges that got you respect in the can, and he had charges that get you hurt or killed in jail. It wasn't until we got back to the training school that Reds would know I was committed that day and knew his secret. I saw his eyes fill with fear when they assigned me to that housing unit. He had two choices: he could call me a liar, in which case I could call his hand by asking for his copy of charging documents (the defendant always gets a copy), or he could ask me to keep his secret in exchange for favors.

His approach was to ask me to keep his secret. As a shot caller, he could get me extra food, easy jobs and part of any contraband that came on the unit. We were allowed to smoke back then, but if drugs came on the unit, I was to get a piece of the action. He further agreed that if I kept his secret, I would be next in line for the shot callers spot once he went home or transferred. I listened to his pitch without saying a word. My silence had him offering me more favors and, of course, he assured me he was innocent. I knew I could have all he was offering if I just took his spot as shot caller, but my brain was calculating the positives and negatives. It was Friday, and I would take the weekend to think things over. Saturday and Sunday were visiting days, and my parents came every Sunday with two cartons of cigarettes and a handful of pills. I would eat the pills in the visiting room and go back stoned. They would strip search me and all that, but it was a waste of time, and to be honest, the security didn't seem to care that people were getting drugs on the weekends—it kept things quiet, I guess. The guys who brought drugs back had to cut the shot callers in or suffer a beat down.

This particular Sunday, I had taken five Percodan in the visiting room and a couple Valium, so I was feeling pretty good by the time I made it back to the section. After visits, I was watching things unfold. I knew one boy came back with lots of powder coke and pills. Now, I wasn't interested in the coke, but I was supposed to be cut in on everything that came in. Of course, Reds got greedy immediately.

Reds, Marked Money and the boy bringing the drugs back had disappeared into the locker room and reappeared in a few minutes with a bad case of the sniffles. I approached Reds. He knew I wasn't happy and was trying to get me away from Marked Money in case I said something. He said, "It was just a small piece; I got you on the next one."

I pushed straight past him and said, "Hey, Money, do you know you're getting high with a baby raper?"

Marked Money was a streetwise kid with an athletic build and a gold-toothed smile; slow to anger, but seriously dangerous when provoked.

Let me take a moment to talk about the juvenile system. While it is a prison for those under the age of 18—and yes, many kids, including me, have earned their spot in one of these places—it's also a place where so many could be saved if anyone cared. This is the place where we can start educating our youth instead of warehousing bodies and creating future convicts. We can provide counseling and education. Early intervention is super important and could be a lifesaver for so many. We have too many people with the lock-'em-up-and-throw-away-the-key mentality. But back to the story.

"What are you talking about?" Marked Money asked in a serious tone.

"Ask Reds," I said, and walked into the locker room.

Mark and Reds followed. Reds had practiced what he'd say, but the words were tumbling out and falling flat as Mark looked him squarely in the eyes. "My step sister set me up, I never touched her."

Reds pleaded his case, but Marked Money remained unreadable as he walked away. No words were exchanged between Reds and me, he knew he messed up.

In the morning, I walked into the main rec hall and shouted, "A-side, line up!" Everybody looked at Reds, who wasn't moving. I walked over to him and said, "Line up for chow." He slowly walked over and got in line, and the murmuring immediately started. There was a changing of the guard, so to speak, and now was the time for anyone to challenge me, I looked to the staff member who walked away to attend to other duties while the politics of a boys prison played out. Whenever there was movement outside the building, you had to count off, and the shot callers made sure that count didn't get messed up. I walked to the front of the line. "Count it off!!!" Just like that I was the new shot caller.

My point to this story is that I learned quite a bit in reform school, but the one thing I didn't learn was any reform. What it did was take my fear of jail away. I now knew that even though this wasn't the big time, I could not only survive with my criminal peers, I could thrive. I hadn't learned one thing about addiction or about getting a job. I only learned how to be a better prisoner of my own addiction. My addiction would only grow now that I was back on the streets with a little reputation as a bad boy. But the truth was, I was headed for terrible times. In Narcotics Anonymous, they say addiction brings three things: jails, institutions, or death, and I've found that to be very true.

Throughout my drug abuse, I was in many jails and institutions and got about as close to death as a person can and still live to tell about it.

Feeding the Monster

I was back home after serving a year in a juvenile jail. I played on the notoriety of having been "away" and really turned my bad ass on high. Please understand that I was raised in a household where all the values are twisted, and that's why today I'm able to understand the gang mentality. When you grow up in a house where law enforcement is the enemy and breaking the law is not only acceptable but expected and favored, you get some twisted thoughts and morals. I know people—or at least some people—who don't believe one can be a product of his environment, but I'm here to tell you when you come up in the house that hell built, you become the devil's best boy, like it or not! Add drugs to that brew, and you get the perfect recipe for disaster. And that's exactly where I was headed, no brakes, no detours, just 100 miles per hour toward destruction. A perfect storm was brewing, and I was at the eye of it.

Things around me were spinning out of control, and I couldn't see the forest for the trees. I really can't blame the neighborhood I grew up in—some very good people grew up right next to me, but my values and view of the world were twisted. I chose to associate with like-minded people; those who were into drugs and on the fringes of society. But here's just how fucked up I was at that point in my life—I believed that the people who worked 9 to 5 were on the fringes of society. They were the outsiders, not me and my merry band of misfits. Life was a long party filled with faceless women, drunken fights and drug-fueled marathon sex sessions. Life was spring break, and I was the king. I had lots of high-grade drugs from my dad the dope dealer and my mother the cancer patient. Money was abundant, and I had more than a few friends willing to help me spend my disposable income. I'd be lying if I said it wasn't fun back then, going to rock concerts, partying till dawn with the dancers from Havenplace and Sportsman's Lounge. I had the drugs they wanted; they had the bodies and loose morals I wanted. My entourage was growing in the city and life was fun, but then came an introduction that would lead me straight into the depths of hell.

I wanted this book to include so much that got left out of my first book, *A Junkie's Nightmare: Coming Clean*, but if you haven't read it, then I have to repeat some info. This was the period of time after training school and before my father was murdered. I had done tons of drugs and had even shot up or injected drugs, but heroin hadn't really come into play. Once it did, it changed everything. The party was coming to an end, yet I couldn't see that it was now beyond my control, I still believed I could quit drugs at any time, and that only losers got addicted because they weren't strong enough to handle the dope. Me, I was different—I was a man's man; all the women wanted me and men wanted to be like me. This is the lie the drugs tell you in the beginning, and it's so easy to be fooled into believing you're in control. But the realization that the drugs were in control would come soon enough. Unfortunately, by then, I didn't know how to change. I just assumed this was the life for me; the hand I had been dealt, so to speak.

After my father's murder and my introduction to heroin came one of my worst withdrawals. I've quit cold turkey in a prison cell, but coming off a hundred-dollar-a-day heroin habit is as close to hell as I ever want to get. By the time they get you from the precinct to city jail, you're already in full withdrawal, and you're not the only one. There are many people kicking when they first come in. Some will try to help by giving you their fruit, but jail is full of predators and someone is watching to see if you have anything worth stealing. Others are hoping to get your food because eating is out of the question for the next few days. No one wants you in their cell because there's no sleeping, and you'll be shitting and throwing up for at least three days. The guards have seen it so many times that you can't expect sympathy from them. The best thing to do is shut your mouth and let the days pass the best you can. You are defenseless, so it's best to stay out of everyone's way and take lots of hot showers, if possible.

I'm going to fast forward a few years to when my addiction to speedballs (a concoction of heroin and cocaine injected directly into the vein) was at an all-time high. Things went from bad to worse, and the drugs were in full control by now. One of my worst experiences was over a simple shoplifting charge! I was trying to fund a hundred-to-a-hundred-and-fifty-dollar-a-day speedball habit, and stealing from stores was doing the trick. But I didn't have a car, and I was getting known in the stores, so getting money was getting tougher and tougher. I went into a store where I had a bad feeling, but I needed money so I stole a few sets of expensive sheets. Security was on me, just waiting for me to walk out the door. As soon as I stepped out, there were three security guards on me. They had seen me stealing before and were waiting for me this time.

The cop who came to pick me up was a real asshole and

things went bad from the start. He put handcuffs on as tight as possible, and when I asked him to loosen them, he told me they weren't built for comfort. I told him they weren't intended as a torture device either, and then things got ugly. It was a shoplifting pinch, yet this cop was treating me really bad. He told me to turn around after our little discussion about handcuffs. I thought he was going to loosen them up a bit, but he grabbed them and clamped them down as tight as they would go, laughing at how clever he was. I called him an asshole, and he banged my head off the roof of the squad car while putting me in the back. When we got to the police station, I told the cop that was booking me that I had a syringe and spoon in my jacket because he was going to search me, and if a cop gets stuck, you're getting the ass-whipping of a lifetime.

The booking cop chewed the arresting officer out for not bagging the needle and cooker, putting me higher on his shit list. Then the booking cop let him have it 'cause it took five minutes to uncuff me. My hands were purple from a lack of circulation, and I had deep lines in my wrists where the metal bit into my flesh. So the booking cop made the arresting officer finish booking me in. I got to look at the paperwork while he was in another room getting fingerprint cards, and this clown charged me with theft under $300, drug paraphernalia and the best one, resisting arrest! So while the officer had his head turned, I stole the evidence bag. When he put me in the cell block, I flushed it. That little cop was furious when he came in the cell block and I said, "Lose something, officer?" The other cops laughed, and he got even angrier, so he took me to the commissioner and they put a $50,000 bail on me for what was the theft of less than $300. Seems fair, huh?

When they took me to the county jail, secure in the fact I wasn't making bail, withdrawal set in fast. Since they didn't have a bed for me, I was given a plastic portable bed that inmates called a "boat." On that boat, I flopped and flipped like a dying fish for seven straight days. Other inmates picked up my 150 lb. frame and carried me to the shower, where I was too weak to do anything but let hot water run on me while holding myself up. Every muscle cramped and every joint ached, but they gave me absolutely no medical attention till other inmates found a decent cop and told him I might die from dehydration. You know it's bad when other cons are merciful, and I wish I knew them to thank them and the cop for getting me to medical. I could hear the medical personnel discussing how bad a case I was. They gave me fluids and some pills that helped very little, but just getting fluids back in helped me a lot. In a few hours I was back in the cell block and back on my boat. It took ten days to get over the sickness, and seventeen days to get a full night's sleep. It's hell to pay when you're poor—and much worse when you're addicted and poor!

Into the Abyss

So why am I telling you all this? Because I know people are smart enough to make their own decisions, and I want you to do just that—make up your own mind as to whether I was a piece of shit or a kid raised under horrible conditions and primed to be a perfect candidate for addiction. I want to let you, the reader, draw your conclusions without me coloring in the edges. While others were learning their ABCs, I was learning to spot a fake twenty dollar bill or a marked tool police could trace as a specialty item. Before me, my father sent my brother through a window too big for an adult to squeeze through but big enough for my ten-year-old brother to climb through, shut off the alarm, and open the back door so my father and his guys could rob the place. Yes, we were raised in horrible conditions, but I also had something else against me, a horrible thing lying in wait for me: addiction.

Please don't misunderstand me. I'm not saying that being an addict is a free pass to hurt people, steal from friends and family, or commit crimes at will, but you have to wonder who I could have been if schools taught real-life lessons, or if someone had actually reached out when I took that first weed pinch instead of taking me in a room and belittling me. Here's the sad truth: the system is designed to keep the poor and addicted enslaved. It has become big business, and the addict is the commodity turning the big wheels of commerce.

Nobody held a gun to my head and made me commit a crime, but before long, I was repeating a cycle I just didn't know how to stop. I'd get locked up, and with no high-priced lawyer, I'd get sent to a prison where there were no programs for the addict. So I'd go get healthy lifting weights and eating daily, and then come out of prison swearing to stay off drugs, only to find myself in a shooting gallery within days (and sometimes hours) of my release. From the movies, you may think jail is full of *Oceans Eleven* types and muscle-bound predators, and while there are predators and the occasional master criminal, that's not what makes up the general population of the prison. Mostly it's twentysomething-year-old men from various races from all over that particular state who share one common thread— being poor, with 90 % or better having addiction problems.

The most common offender has little to no education and a history of abuse or violence in his home. Not many are rich or come from a rich family. There are a few. One kid stands out in my memory as a victim of drugs, the jail and society at large. Why society? Because every day that we don't write our elected officials and ask them to stop treating addicts as criminals, we are contributing to the death of a sick person. This kid was your typical rich kid who happened to have the disease of addiction. His name was Gabe. His father owned a bunch of stores in the city that catered to the hip-hop crowd, and Gabe was handed everything until addiction got him thrown out of his father's house and he began boosting (retail theft) to support a ridiculously large speedball habit. His parents had bailed him out time after time, but Gabe never took it seriously. He always had daddy's money and lawyers to run to his rescue.

Well, Gabe and I came to Baltimore County Detention Center on the same day for shoplifting, Gabe got a $20,000 bail because he had three open cases and the commissioner was getting tired of seeing him. The intake process at county jail is an all-day deal that seriously would sap a strong person's strength but it's agonizing for someone in withdrawal. You're put in a bullpen that looks like a fishbowl with twenty to thirty other of your not-so-closest friends for hours while the cops throw paper clips at one another and do 'paperwork.' Then you come out three or four at a time to get strip-searched and put your belongings in a bag. Then they put you in the shower and give you lice and crab-killing soap before issuing you a bedroll and a blue jumpsuit three sizes too big. You're then hustled to another bullpen to await a trip to medical. You go to medical and plead for something for withdrawal, but they tell you "We don't treat addicts." Then it's off to your assigned tier. Gabe and I went through the process together, and the whole time he was bitching to get processed so he could get to a phone and call his dad to bail him out. As for me, I knew what my next ten days looked like, but Gabe just knew he'd be back to his drugs in a few hours.

As we got to 2A (a receiving tier), he ran to the phone without putting his bedroll in the cell, it wasn't long before everyone could hear him screaming and demanding that his dad get the bail bondsman. His parents had had enough of Gabe's promises, and while they were accepting multiple collect calls, they refused to bail him out. Over the next few days while I kicked a habit, Gabe cried, promised, threatened, begged and said anything to get his parents to bail him out. Finally, it seemed he broke through their resolve. He got off the phone and came over to where I was laying on the floor and said, "Man, they're calling the bail bondsman now, but I gotta go to rehab."

I congratulated him and told him at least the rehab will medicate him. He was overjoyed and told me he'd give anything to sleep for a few hours while they bailed him out. He paced the tier for the next few hours, but as it got closer to lock-in time, he still wasn't called for bail release. He went back over to the phone, but it was one of the shortest phone calls I'd seen him make, I knew when he hung up and headed toward me it was bad news. He sat down next to me and said, "I can't believe they put a block on my calls." I was sad for Gabe, but I knew his parents had been through hell with him because I know what I put mine through. It's not that we want to hurt those who love us, but the compulsion to do the drugs takes priority over everything else, and until you get treatment and find out what the problems are, well, you just tear through people's lives like a tornado.

Gabe grabbed my shoulder and said goodbye, which I found weird, but I figured he was going to go lay in his bunk and shed those self-loathing tears that only a fellow junkie understands. He went to his cell, and when you have to use the toilet or don't want your cells to come in, you cover the thick Plexiglass that's in the cell doors at BCDC with a strip of toilet paper or a towel. I didn't notice that the door was still covered until it was about ten minutes to lock-in when I heard Gabe's cellmate say, "Damn, he's been shitting for two hours. That boy is dope sick!"

I walked over to Gabe's cell and pulled the door open, Gabe's face was the color of a plumb, and his head looked like it was about to burst. Time moved in slow motion as my brain tried to understand what my eyes were seeing. Gabe had hanged himself with a jail-issue sheet from the air vent in his cell. His feet were just about four inches off the floor. As I rushed into the cell, I must have yelled to the other inmates because as I grabbed Gabe around the waist to try and get the pressure off his neck, others were filling the small area. I could smell death, and it was pretty obvious that Gabe had vacated his bowels. In minutes, the staff had locked all but a few of us in and allowed me and others to get Gabe down, where we brought him out on the tier. Medical worked on him for forty minutes waiting for the ambulance that arrived forty-five minutes later. They wheeled him out with a sheet over him and filled his cell by the next morning. No big loss—just one less junkie, right? Well, I didn't know Gabe well, but maybe his death will have some meaning if this book changes one mind about the way we treat sick people in this country.

Kids like myself, who are messed up on drugs, enter into these places needing drug rehab or some type of treatment and leave there with a degree in crime! They have learned the ins and outs of the system, and jail doesn't scare them anymore because they see it's not like the movies. You house them around dangerous criminals and they become dangerous criminals—and they're coming back to your community! Mr. John Q., they are moving next door with Aunt Linda and Uncle Bill, 'cause Mom don't want that back home around the crowd he was running with when he was arrested. If that don't worry you, how about the fact that six in ten will return to prison within three years! Don't worry, you have good luck—the one that moves next door to you will be that one in a bunch that does well.

I'm not slamming you with ACLU stats to draw some sort of outrage from you. I'm just telling you my observations and the way the facts stack up. More often than not, you have people in jail who have a treatable disease, whether that disease be substance abuse or the dreaded awful luck to be a poor person—both can be treated if they want to treat it, but that would put a lot of people out of work. It would also destroy the slave labor industry, but more on these things later.

I'll just wrap this chapter up by saying the problems that face us in this country will not be alleviated or even addressed if no one shakes things up. For now, the prisons keep getting built, and the prisons keep getting filled! Drug addicts and alcoholics are branded and tossed inside like so many sheep. The rich get richer and the poor get locked up for trying to get their piece of the American Dream.

War on What?

While you and I are sitting here having our morning coffee, I want you to think about the so-called "War on Drugs." Has it been even a little bit successful? In forty years, has anything changed? If you're even the tender age of thirty, do you remember how cheap a gallon of gas was when you started driving? OK, how much was a pack of cigarettes back when people used to smoke? While inflation has doubled, tripled and quadrupled, do you know how much a bag of dope has increased? Would you believe this—not only did the price of heroin not go up, the quality has gotten better and the price has gone down!!!! The same for cocaine, despite stiffer sentences and mandatory sentencing. Even though the news shows record seizures of tons of drugs, and even though we're building bigger prisons and handing out more and more time, the drugs still flow into our country like running water.

I've never seen a poppy field or a coca plant growing in East Baltimore, but on nearly every corner there's an open

-air drug market. There's millions of addicts walking the street, and there's millions more addicted housewives and prescription junkies visiting a doctor handing out increasingly stronger drugs with impunity. We are taking our poor people and locking them up in what some consider modern-day plantations while drug company execs enjoy unprecedented bonuses.

If you watch the nightly news around election time, there will be some momo on there telling you if you elect him he's going to make your streets safe to walk on. Just who is he talking to? Ask anyone who lives in the inner city how safe they feel (and please don't make this a racial issue because poor white folks are going to jail at a never-before-seen rate)! The war clearly isn't on drugs, because if it were, any rational human would have to admit that we surrendered a long time ago. The war is on poor people.

I'm not one of these people who see a conspiracy around every corner, or thinks that I have all the answers. By the same token, I don't need a brick wall to fall on me to see that something is very wrong with our (their) system. I've been in that system and subject to information a lot of people just won't believe about our government, so I know that as I write this, people will claim I'm a liberal, or that I'm just trying to sell books, but I have seen the ugly face of this war and I know who it's directed at. I'm just pointing out some facts—feel free to google them or look into them because I stand behind every word.

While serving that thirty month sentence (by the way, my record was full of drug beefs by then, and I was in jail on a drug-related charge), I was offered no programs and was only able to volunteer for AA meetings. I went to one meeting, and there was no one from the outside to run it, so it was run by the convicts and consisted of a couple guys who went to the meeting to pass out dope and girlie books, I left ten minutes into the "meeting." I didn't have enough time for this program, and I'd just missed the sign-up for that program. What they could offer me (since I was minimum security) was a move up the street to the road crew building where I could make 85 cents a day and get five days a month shaved off my sentence to go out and clean up parks or pick up trash on the roadways. I would be under police escort, but no chains or prison stripes. My first day on the job, I shoveled rock salt all day for the trucks to come out in the snow. I went back to my cell with blisters on my hands and the satisfaction that I had made 85 cents that day. Who said crime doesn't pay?

Now, there were other jobs where you could make the big bucks—the broom shop workers made three dollars a day, the auto shop that fixed all the officers' private cars made three a day, and it was rumored that the meat-cutting shop guys made upwards of five dollars a day. That's not an hour, people—that's a day! Meanwhile, the guards are selling furniture made by the prisoners or having their buddy's car worked on at the prison garage, and God only knows how many steer went out that back door. The cops and the wardens of these jails all collecting kickbacks off the backs of the convicts. Now you may say, "But isn't meat cutting or working on cars a good trade they can take home and produce out in the free world?"

Well, yes and no. Here's the thing: you're not taught to build a table—you may be the guy who sands the wooden legs, and each step has its own task, but never is a worker taught the entire skill.

Say they are building a table, for the sake of illustration. One guy is the sander, another is the stainer, another is the guy who planes the wood and another is an assembly guy. I'm not sure where one can get a job just sanding table tops. Furthermore, you have to have a large sentence to get in the shop. You may go on a five-year waiting list just to be considered for one of these coveted positions. The guys who sweep the tier make 85cents a day while the kitchen guys enjoy the lucrative $1.15 a day and all the food they can steal!

So with no counseling and no job skills, I returned to the streets a year later and was rearrested on parole violation and multiple felonies all revolving around drugs within months of my release. Listen, folks, I'm not saying I was a good person who was wrongly convicted. I admit I did some terrible shit to get high, but if jails and prisons are houses of correction, then where's the correction? Where are the programs? Where's the job training? They say there's no money. Well, what happened to those millions of dollars that were seized in the "drug war?"

I know you've seen the "get-tough" politicians and judges talking about how enough is enough. The time has come to step up the war, but here's some simple truths, folks: the war isn't working, it never has, and I'm not so sure it was ever intended to. It's a new way to create a slave workforce for the rich to get richer while the poor break their backs. If you try to get a little bigger slice of the American Dream, they will seize your assets, take your family away and lock you in the hottest corner of hell. They tell you this is all in the name of keeping you safe. Do you feel safe???

Who's Profiting?

OK, so who is profiting from locking people up? Well, a lot of people, but let's start with the obvious. Say a kid starts selling nickel bags, then moves up to selling substantial amounts for a few years. The law will come in and take everything from him, and the law has a long reach—if anything is in his name, whether it came from drug money or not, is seized. They can even take his mother's house, and the real hit is the police don't have to prove the mother's house was bought with drug money—she has to prove it wasn't! So they take the jewelry, houses, and cars, and if there's any left over, well, the lawyers get that. That money goes directly to the police, and what they don't steal for their individual use goes to fund these paramilitary groups with weapons and tactical gear to take down more drug dealers. Some of these SWAT Teams are completely funded by the seizures they take, so don't believe they don't look for the best targets. It's worth noting that the courts give these groups lots of leverage to use "tactics" to create a larger bottom line (money), even allowing the cops to take gold teeth plates. Many of these police are the real "run and gun" types who love coming to work to "suit up and bust some heads."

So the dealer gets his stuff taken and goes to prison, where his freedom is not his own, and that's it, right? The system rehabilitates him and returns him to society, never to offend again, huh? We both know that's junk. No, he is locked up along with thousands who are in there for the crimes I mentioned earlier—shoplifting, petty theft and possession—which are crimes that beg to be recognized as being directly related to addicts. No counseling, no programs, just a menial "job" and the rec hall to play cards. If they do have "job training," like when Boeing turned the Washington state reformatory into its "factory" for machining parts, they pay an inmate seven bucks an hour, but his "take–home" pay is less than a dollar because the prison makes these working inmates pay rent, as well as percentages to cover court costs and fines, plus an additional percentage to victims of violent crime. The prisoner works 10-12 hours a day, the company doesn't have to pay him when there's no work (like they would a free world employee), and there's no medical or sick leave. And if the inmate gets hurt on the job, the state picks up the tab. That is to say, the taxpayers pick up the tab!

You can't tell me there aren't backroom meetings and thick envelopes of cash kicked back to jailers who make "employees" readily available. The saddest part is if you ask the inmate about the job, he will give the jail high praise 'cause a dollar an hour is much better than 85 cents a day. I'm not picking on Boeing—there are many companies using modern slaves, whether they're paying them a dollar a day to make clothes or computer parts, or locking illegal immigrants in their stockrooms so they can't leave. If these prisons weren't such moneymakers, why would we see so many private prisons popping up? I may dedicate a chapter to private prisons just because their short history is a bloody one. The main problem is ineffective staffing in private prisons. Putting a guy in a uniform after an eight- hour "training" course and putting him in charge of prisoners is a recipe for disaster and has ended in disaster on many occasions. However, let's get back to our subject: profits.

It's one thing for a guard to get the guys in the prison shop to fix his alternator, but it's another to funnel thousands of dollars out the back door. Yet, you have this going on every day. The state gives so much money to each institution, depending on the number of prisoners, that it costs something like $45,000 per year to house an inmate. So it's to the jailer's advantage to have his prison filled to capacity. Any corners he can cut is money is his pocket, literally, and the first corners to be cut are the very corners that would keep an inmate from returning to prison: education and drug treatment. Recidivism is not bad news to anyone trying to keep the beds full to capacity. Recidivism is profit.

Now, you may be saying, "OK, Freddie Jay, they lock people up and work the hell out of them and take most of their money, but that's the life they chose, and it doesn't affect me, so to hell with them!" I understand you're fed up with crime, but this affects us all in a huge way. Not only are the jails releasing untreated addicts back to your neighborhood to commit more property crimes, but the Boeing job I mentioned above used to be some union worker's $35 an hour job lost to prison slave labor. People love to complain about immigrants coming in to the country and working for pennies on the dollar, but it's more than likely you're losing your job to the local prison and not the immigrant!!!

This is big business, and what big business cares about is money, plain and simple. If they can fill orders, pay low wages and show record profits, many of these execs would climb into bed with Satan himself, and some do! I know we all would like to believe that corruption and backroom deals are a thing of the past, but believe me, it's alive and well, and it's you, me and the so-called middle class that pays the cost. I use the term middle-class loosely because the United States really is becoming a nation of either the very rich or the very poor, and as much as I hate to admit it, I'll always be a second-class citizen in the eyes of the powers that be. However, to be one of the profiteers of this game, I have to either take part in the imprisonment of my fellow man or turn a blind eye while others do well. I prefer my position in life, so I'll close this chapter with the Gospel of Mark 8:36—"For what shall it profit a man if he should gain the whole world, yet lose his own soul!"

What Can Be Done?

I don't have all the answers, but I can see that something is very wrong, and there are some things that can be done. There are organizations that help prisoners, but these programs usually involve volunteers working with limited resources because they are funded by donations with no assistance from the state or federal government. Also, a lot of companies that use the slave labor of prisoners refuse to hire ex-cons—now isn't that hypocrisy at its pinnacle?! People point to prison work as job training, but the inmates are being trained for jobs they can't get when they get out! When convicts come out of prison and are given help with housing and employment, the chances of them returning to prison drops significantly; when you add drug education, those numbers drop to the low teens.

It costs a lot to lock a person up. Some people estimate it at 60,000 per year, per person, and considering there's more than 2,000,000 people locked up in the United States, that's serious tax money going to warehouse humans. This money could be spent in much better ways to keep people out of jail and make them productive members of society. If we spent money to educate people and treat their addictions, we could seriously reduce property crimes and nuisance crimes, as well as shoplifting and petty theft. Every time you walk in a store, you're paying the mark up on every item you purchase because of retail theft. Like it or not, this problem is dropped squarely in each of our laps. I'm not talking about the issues "out there" or their issues—I'm talking about our problems confronting us today!

You can even put prisoners to work, but provide real-world job training and education. Teach them real-world things like how to dress for an interview and how to fill out an application online. Many prisoners hitting the streets are computer illiterate. And then there's the big mother of them all—drug education. Education and drug treatment work, and this is what's needed in our prisons. Let's prepare people for society. Look, I'm not a politician, and I'm not some brilliant doctor or professor, but you don't have to be any of those things to see the old way isn't working and that a major overhaul is needed!

As I write, the powers that be are cutting drug dealers'

sentences simply because there's too much overcrowding. The sentencing commission is going to session to address concerns with mandatory sentencing, and the Justice Department has said it will no longer pursue mandatory minimums for nonviolent drug crimes. This is a step in the right direction, but there is still much to be done, and I, for one, think that decriminalizing drugs could be the way to go. Countries like Portugal, which is at the forefront of experimental drug policies, have had great success when treating the addict while still going after those who traffic in large amounts.

Just think of how much money and resources we could save if we focused our attention on the cartels and the bankers that launder the drug money? How much more productive would our society be if we didn't have ten million "criminals" who have trouble finding jobs, getting credit or voting because of possession charges or charges directly related to drug use? I'm in no way saying we should open the gates of all the prisons and let everyone run free. What I am saying is we need to open our eyes and start seeing that the War on Drugs is a complete and utter failure. Let's cut our losses, treat the victims of this war, and reposition ourselves to make a difference for future generations.

Decriminalizing drugs would also help decrease the spread of infectious diseases like a decrease in hepatitis C and HIV. Addicts would come forward if the fear of jail were removed to be treated for these and other diseases, allowing health officials to get a better handle on these things. If drugs were legal, addicts would have access to clean needles, and this would cut down on the passing of blood-born diseases.

While in prison, on my second major incarceration) there was a guy we called Johnny B Good, and this guy was incredibly likable. He even made the meanest of the mean crack up. If you were having an off-day, Johnny B Good would come past your cell, walking on his hands to get a laugh out of you—that was just his nature. He was in prison on his umpteenth theft conviction, and if there was dope in the jail, Johnny knew who had it, how much there was and what the quality was. At this time, my mother was bringing me heroin in the jail, and Johnny was my best customer. He had a guy upstairs bringing him syringes out of the infirmary, but no one really knew where those needles came from. Half the time, they got passed around till they were about as sharp as a nail and you had no idea who had them before you, so I wouldn't touch them unless I had my nurse connection get them for me.

One day, Johnny B Good didn't come out for dinner, so, I went past his cell and asked him if he was alright. He laughed and said he had a coughing fit and just didn't feel good, so he was going to lay in for the night. Johnny never got out of bed again. That night his cells noticed him making funny sounds and tried to wake him. When Johnny wouldn't respond, he called the guard who took two hours to get a stretcher down to Johnny's cell, Johnny fell into a coma and died two days later. Johnny had full blown AIDS and didn't even know it. There was a mad rush of people getting tested the next few days, including me. I had seen others that I figured were sick, and even though I didn't share needles with Johnny, it hit close to home, so to speak, for me.

I've seen firsthand what drugs do. I've seen the insides of our prisons, and there's one thing more dangerous than the prisons and the people who run them. More dangerous than the big businesses that profit from slave labor. And that is the public apathy. I know it's easy to turn your back on prisoners; it's easy to view drug addicts as people who create their own conditions, but here's the truth: we are all connected, and people in prison are people who made a mistake and deserve a chance at the American Dream. We can change this. We can contact our elected officials and hold them accountable. We can volunteer to organizations that help prisoners or give financial support to worthy groups committed to helping ex-cons. If you own a business, give an ex-con a job; if you're an employee ask your company to sponsor someone who deserves a chance. If you think about it, we are saving ourselves!

Are you aware that the Fraternal Order of Police has publicly come out against medical pot? Along with the FOP, many other police organizations have openly come out against medical marijuana. They're not in the medical field, so why would law enforcement weigh in on medical marijuana? Let me tell you why—MONEY! Sure, it's about job loss and the fear the states will need less cops if you allow medical pot, but the big issue is the bottom line: the almighty dollar. No states are exempt, but since I have a link, let me take on California, The Golden States motto, Eureka, goes back to the Gold Rush, but could just as easily be applied to the amount the state has made on confiscating money, houses and cars from people in possession of marijuana. How much have they made? Would you believe over $180 million since '02?

Cali Cops Take Home $181 Million Worth of Loot in Their War Against Medical Marijuana

Alternet http://www.alternet.org/drugs/cali-cops-take-home-181-million-worth-loot-their-war-against-medical-marijuana

Open your computer and look this stuff up. It's very real, and it's right in front of us. I don't want to turn this book into an argument for or against medical pot, but it's certainly worth noting that law enforcement doesn't care one way or the other about the medical benefits of marijuana—they care about the revenue it creates. It doesn't matter if someone gets relief from a terrible disease like multiple sclerosis. It's still being researched, but many of today's "legal" drugs used to treat MS are not tolerated well by patients and have lots of side effects. Does law enforcement think about these things when they come out against medical pot? The answer is no—it's all about the dollar.

This one issue shows the attitude of law enforcement as a whole. If they aren't considering people with a disease like MS, imagine how far down addicts and alcoholics rate.

Falling Through the Cracks

I was back in prison in Hagerstown, MD, for trying to pass a fraudulent prescription for Dilaudid (a potent pain killer popular among heroin addicts for its similar effects, and because it can be crushed and injected) when I met a 19-year-old boy named Zachary. He was from one of those small towns on the eastern shore of Maryland notorious for giving huge sentences. Zack got twenty-five years for breaking and entering. He was a young dope addict who had been in lots of trouble from the age of twelve or so, and the judge nailed him with back-to-back consecutive sentences for multiple B&Es. He was a goofy, likable kid who loved to play, which wore on my nerves from time to time, but he was always laughing and joking. He got in trouble buying heroin with a dude on my tier. Lonny threatened Zack, and he came running to me. I wasn't Mr. Badass, but if you read *A Junkie's Nightmare: Coming Clean,* you know I was a seasoned veteran by now who knew how to survive the prison atmosphere. I went to the guy and talked on Zack's behalf. You would think he would learn his lesson, but not Zack!

Anyway I go to Lonny and talk him into cutting Zack a break, and he cuts the bill by 75% for immediate payment which I pay for him with the understanding that if he gets in trouble again, he's on his own.

That should be where the story ends, but it gets really convoluted from here. I guess a month or so passed when I went by the rec hall to find Zack back at the table playing cards with Lonny and his boys. Zachary was so high he could barely hold his cards. I really couldn't believe how dumb this boy was. Zack saw me and came over. "Man, I'm up 10 dollars," he gushed as I looked over his shoulder to see Lonny flash a wide smile, I just shook my head and walked away without a word. Soon enough, Zack was back in my cell with a sad tale. Looking back, I'm so sorry I didn't help him because I thought I knew what was coming, but no one could've seen the events about to unfold.

It seems Zack went to a white guy who offered to pay his bill. This guy everyone called Breezy (for reasons unknown) was known for tricking young guys to move into his cell where he would sexually assault them. Zack was just dumb enough to fall into the trap. To make this already long story a little shorter, I'll wrap this up. Zack moved in with Breezy, who assaulted him the first night in the cell. Zack goes to the infirmary to get his ass stitched up, and afterward is put on a protective custody. In my opinion this kid could've been so much more, but some "get tough" judge gave him an outrageous sentence, so he was put in a dangerous prison. He was a dope addict who could've been helped through some intense treatment. Again, I don't think he should have received a free pass for breaking into people's houses, but come on, twenty-five years in a dangerous prison where he was raped? The last time I saw him, he was wearing eye shadow and short shorts. He became a full-fledged, practicing homosexual. I don't know if those tendencies were always there beneath the surface, or if this was his way of dealing with what happened to him. What I do know is he came into prison a goofy kid who loved to play, and he will leave there someone very different. Please understand, I'm not against anyone's lifestyle choices, but I don't think this was a choice—he was the victim of the disease of addiction.

Now, Zack's just one case, but I've seen so many just like him, I'll let you draw your own conclusions. He will get passed around like a cheap bottle of wine and be discarded just as easy. No one can say what Zachary could've been, but I know this, prison isn't the place for people who suffer with the disease of addiction. At least not for crimes like shoplifting, theft, or victimless crimes such as possession. I agree that being an addict isn't a defense for murder or rape or some other horrendous crime, but I think so many of these crimes could be prevented with early intervention and education.

What Will I Do to Help?

First, I wrote this book to get this message out. Then, I plan to go on a speaking tour. I will speak in any school, college, or institution to try and educate people about the disease of addiction. I'm not asking you to do things I won't do myself—I'm asking you to write your elected officials and ask them what programs are available to prisoners in your state. Talk to the people at your kids' school and ask them about what kind of education your kids receive on real world issues. Talk to your kids— create a time for the family to get together and discuss what's going on in everybody's life. Kids need to know they can trust someone; someone they can talk to. Right now, so many people are at a cross road, but if they just have a person they can trust to go to, it could be the very difference between life and death. I'm not giving you dramatics here—I'm giving you the facts. I know them because I lived them. I've been in a prison cell working for 85 cents a day, and I know what prison offers an addict:

very little.

There's finally a governor (in Vermont) who wants to treat addiction in the medical field, and I applaud him, because it was politicians who started the whole "lock them up and throw away the key" mentality. Nancy Regan and her "Just Say No" bullshit made it seem like people had a choice, but let me tell you something: people aren't dying in record numbers by choice. No one chooses to be the outcast of society, living on the fringes of life, existing off the scraps of others. The veterans who served with honor didn't choose to be curled up tonight on a cold park bench with a bottle in his pocket. Most addicts would do anything to change their station in life. Most, like myself, didn't know how to get clean, and more importantly, don't know how to stay clean. I certainly didn't. I really believed there was no way out for a person like me.

These well-meaning politicians with their half-assed, uninformed ideas like Just Say No or the DARE program lead the general public to believe that addicts have a choice in the matter. Believe me, Mrs. Reagan, if I could have just said no I would have. You can say that the Just Say No campaign is from the '80s, so why am I still talking about it? But think about it—our mindset has changed very little since then. The belief that addicts choose their lifestyle and should be locked up is evident by the soaring incarceration numbers and the lack of funding for addiction education and treatment. If you bought this book, either you or someone you love has been affected by the drug epidemic, and you are not alone. Drugs are everywhere, and people who would never use heroin or cocaine will gladly take a prescription to the pharmacy for the ever-increasing strength of hydrocodone, a drug in the opiate family that produces the exact same euphoria and has the same addictive properties as smack! We must change our thinking about drugs and drug addiction. It's ridiculous that we are locking up people in record numbers, but if you have a white coat and an M.D. behind your name, you can destroy lives with impunity.

I watched someone I love go from being able to only take half of a five milligram Percocet to taking upwards of 150 milligrams each day over a yearlong period. Now, I'm not suggesting that we leave people in pain or lock up every doctor that prescribes an opiate; I am saying we need our doctors to look a little more closely at people's history and stop with the cookie-cutter approach to health care.

Who can blame the doctors when they are courted by the drug companies? It's amazing that most people don't know that their doctor is being rewarded by the drug companies for pushing their drugs. It's backroom politics at its worst.

I'm not talking about problems that are "out there." This isn't an inner city problem or a black problem—it's our problem!! No matter your background, lifestyle, race, color or creed, this affects you! When you go to your local store and buy a pack of razors, you're paying a marked-up price put in place to compensate for theft. Put a pretty name on it—call it leakage or loss control—but the truth is you're paying extra for others to steal it! We need to start asking the right questions of our elected officials and lawmakers; we need to hold them accountable and stop allowing our tax dollars to be squandered on stupid projects or over-priced toilet seats. For those of you who didn't hear the news story, the toilet seats on Air Force One, the president's plane, cost over $400! If you doubt me, go ahead and google it. I'm sorry, the price was $640.00. My mistake (**Air Force Cost for Toilet Cover Is Criticized** — *The Los Angeles Times*). At any rate, it's just one example of waste in government.

I'm not looking to take on the government or any one politician—I just want to change minds about the sick and suffering amongst us, and I care so much because I have been the sick, the outcast, the imprisoned... and all my troubles revolved around drugs in some shape or form. I know there are those who are convinced that addicts choose to do drugs, and it's those people I want to reach and ask them to consider that maybe, just maybe, these folks suffer from a disease they didn't ask for.

I have watched the so-called good people get addicted to drugs. Right now, there's a housewife running to three different doctors to get different prescriptions. There's a professional popping a handful of Percocet before going into the boardroom, and there's a network of women calling their girlfriends –and the conversation may go like this:

First Woman: "Did you get your Xanax yet?"

Second Woman: "No, I go to the doctor on the fifth. I have a few Valium."

First Woman: "Great. I'll pick them up on the way to get Janet from school."

Second Woman: "OK. If you go past the liquor store, grab me a box of wine."

You may think the above example is far-fetched, but more and more, people are slammed to the gills on wine and prescription drugs. In some cases, they are not only taking care of their own kids, but taking care of your kids.

School bus drivers and teachers aren't exempt, and

neither are law enforcement officers or professionals. It's really sad to see how far the prescription drug problem runs in this country, and the worst part is that some of these people look down on a heroin addict and refuse to see that they are suffering from the very same disease. This reality only comes home when they run out of the precious prescription that keeps them from going out of their mind.

Let's keep it moving with some more examples of life for a junkie.

Good Gone Bad

OK, time for another story from the Freddie Jay Files. We'll call this guy Freddie. OK, it's me! Growing up in a household that was full of violence, drugs, drinking and fighting doesn't usually produce a child with good manners, but if you talked to any of my neighbors from back then, I guarantee they would describe a soft-spoken, skinny kid who always said, "Yes, ma'am" and "Yes, sir" and always seemed to be looking at his feet. My mother got sick when I was just a little guy, and I was her full-time, live-in nurse. I went to all her chemotherapy treatments, as well as cobalt treatments. I missed a lot of time from school, and at one point, had a tutor coming into the house. I would go down and talk with the social workers and staff members, who I was on a first-name basis with at Greater Baltimore Medical Center. Everyone knew me, from the doctors to the janitors, and they all liked the boy with the sad eyes. Some realized I had much more on my plate then a boy my age should have, but 1976 was a different time, and people tended to mind their own business—and those who tried to intervene were quickly dealt with by my father, who wanted to keep selling his wife's pain medicine and keep his son as an indentured servant. I was a very quiet and respectful kid, and would stay that way up until the drugs became such a compulsion that I was unable to feed the monster that raged inside me.

I tell this story because I want you to see how easy it is to become an addict if the disease already lives in you. At thirteen, I was like any other kid, except I was on the fast track to prison due to the lack of parenting. By this time, my mother was stoned on one kind of medicine and my dad was selling the other, no one seemed to care that I was coming in with whiskey on my breath—or not coming in at all. I had started drinking with the older crowd, which led to smoking pot, which eventually led to a heroin addiction. Not everyone who picks up a drink or even smokes pot will go on to become a drug addict, but for me, it was a natural progression. In the beginning, it was fun, and every night was a party. But I always had to do more than everyone else. When they were passing out, I was just getting started. . I had access to high-grade narcotics and lots of money—a recipe for disaster if there ever was one.

In the beginning, the drugs allowed me a certain peace.

I wasn't scared that my mom was dying, and I wasn't afraid of my dad's bullying tactics. I didn't consider that I had two brothers pulling long stretches and I was heading in the same direction. You can say I needed a swift kick in the ass—and maybe you're right—but what I needed was for someone to understand me because I didn't understand why I was doing the things I was doing. And the older guys who maybe could have helped me were too busy doing the good drugs I had, or helping me spend my money. I carry no resentment toward those guys, but I do accept it for what it is.

It wasn't long before I was sticking a needle in my arm, and it wasn't long before I became a known heroin addict. That's some label to have, and all before the age of 20!! It's sad, it's pathetic, and I hope it makes you angry because the thought of a teenager shooting dope infuriates me. It can be stopped. We can treat people at a young age without labeling them for the rest of their lives. If we start teaching our kids how to avoid the traps of becoming all that I was—if we listen to all that our kids are saying, and more importantly listen to everything they're not saying—we can reach them before they become a casualty of the failed War on Drugs!

It's so easy to get caught up in the system, and it simply

isn't designed to help or correct people. If you're poor and get in trouble, you're much more likely to get jail time than someone with a lawyer or a team of lawyers—hello, O.J.!

O.J. had a mountain of evidence against him, and his lawyers tore through it bit by bit till the jury only heard Charlie Brown's parents. When he went to court a few years later without those big names, he got sentenced to 20 years over some bullshit! How about the Menendez brothers, those boys who killed their parents in Beverly Hills! They were just as guilty as the day is long, and while their money held out they got two mistrials. Once the money was gone and the high-priced mouthpiece with it, they were convicted. I have nothing against O.J. or them boys, but I am pointing out two big cases where it's blatantly obvious that money played a huge roll in guilt or innocents—aside from the glaring facts!

My father had a saying—"Money talks and bullshit walks." While my father wasn't exactly eloquent, he does have a point. We see it every day and accept it as business as usual: the rich get richer and the poor get stepped on, and as long as we lay down and take it, the divide will grow. The war on junkies will continue, and more prisons will be built, while the wardens get kickbacks from the slave labor, and we just say, "Thank you, sir! May I have another?"

The environment of prison is one that makes people return to an under-evolved, Neanderthal existence. It pits blacks against whites and brown against the rest, and all for a piece of the scraps that society throws away. A pack of cigarettes that sells for five dollars on the street can range from $40 to $250 behind bars. Dope is brought in by the guards in most institutions, and while the staff watches the visiting room, their coworkers walk right through the front door with the drugs. Everyone knows it, but no one wants to face it. If the powers that be can keep us fighting amongst ourselves, they are more than happy to give us a doggie bag while they walk away with a steak.

In my personal life, I hadn't experienced racism before going to prison. For all my father's faults, one thing he did believe in was equality among the races. We grew up believing people were people to be judged by "the content of their character and not the color of their skin," so it was quite shocking to end up in Hagerstown, where the white guards called people "niggers" and "nigger lovers." But what really was shocking was my first trip to Baltimore City Detention Center. Called "The Jail" by most people from Baltimore, it is easily 95% black and no place for the soft of spirit. It can be a deadly stop for someone without friends or intestinal fortitude, and it's certainly no place to be in withdrawal because you're an easy victim for just about everyone. As luck would have it, I was in the precinct for about twenty days waiting for city police to pick me up on a violation of probation. This was back before they had central booking, and you had to go from a county precinct to a city precinct, and then to city jail. During this time, I had gone through the worst part of withdrawal and was actually feeling pretty good when I went to the city jail on a receiving tier to await trial on a "vop" for... yep, you guessed it... a drug charge.

It was on that tier that I started working out and getting in shape while awaiting placement within the jail. It was my first time in city jail, and the other guys told me if they assign you to "J" Section or "K" Section, just punch the cop in the mouth and go to lock-up right away. They called it "Jumping J" and "Killer K" respectively. Black dudes didn't want to go to these sections, but it was a death sentence for a white guy—the sections were 100 % black, and even the guards who got assigned to these tiers had to piss off a superior to draw duty on one of them.

So the day comes for transfers from receiving to tiers that will be your home till you go to court. The guard informed the twenty of us that no one was going to "J"

Section and only one going to "K," but he didn't give you your section till you were standing in front of it. I had a one in twenty chance of going to the infamous section, and I felt pretty good about my chances. I mean, I didn't have a murder charge—I had a simple violation over dirty urine while on probation, and it was about a year old, so I felt pretty good, at least until the numbers started to dwindle till there were two of us standing there. The guard looked at me and the other dude and says, "One of you is going to The Annex and the other to Killer K!" The Annex was dorms with lots of freedom and room to hustle, and "K" was a nightmare. "Freddie—K Section!" The words hit with a thud to my heart. My stomach got that hollow feeling only fear brings.

Well, there was nowhere to run, so I stepped up to the door when the guards started arguing about putting me in there. "Man, you put him on this section, you might as well bring a body bag!"

The guard working the tier said, "You know it ain't my call. The sergeant gave me a list, and I didn't know he was white till we got here."

I'm looking at both of them like a deer in the headlights. I've done nothing to anyone. I haven't had a fight or a cross word with a single person, and I only had a violation of probation, so why was I being put on a tier with murderers, rapists, and the worst of the worst? All these thoughts were running through my head as the guards finished their discussion and pushed me through the door. I started walking to my cell, but didn't make it before a dude walked up and said, "Hey, white boy, are you crazy? Turn around and tell the police to put you on PC."

I really didn't realize he was trying to help me. "Look..." I began, and before the word was out of my mouth, a punch came from somewhere, and till this day, I'm not sure from where, but white light flashed as a fist found the side of my head. I turned to fight and was bombarded by fists from many directions. The police ran in and broke it up, but now I'm furious. I wasn't being attacked for anything other than being white, and I didn't like it.

The guards tried to help—they really did—but I refused medical, I refused PC and I refused to be run-off the section. I got beat up three times that same night. Surprisingly, no knives or shanks, as they are called in jail, were used. I kept fighting back, and I kept losing. I'd love to tell you I pulled a Jet Li and won the respect of my peers, but that's just not true. By the next morning, I looked like the Elephant Man, but even through the pain and humiliation, I can see where God watched over me. In the morning, I walked out of my cell, and about two cells down, out stepped a guy I knew from the streets. His name was Butchie Shepard, but everyone called him "Six-Nine" because of his size. It took a moment for him to recognize me, but he walked over and a look of true concern creased his brow, "Point out who did this."

Killer 'K'

Butchie had a murder charge, but the witnesses were recanting their stories in a hurry. Butch worked for a drug organization for a guy I'll call "One-Armed Dee," who I also knew from my travels in the drug world. Butchie was Dee's enforcer, collector and, some say, hit man. One day I had pulled up on a corner in East Baltimore to cop some heroin. One-Armed Dee walked over to my car, which was strange, because he was a big dog. He never took money at the street level. But that night, he came over and asked me to give his boy a ride. It was then that I met Butchie. I had heard his name, and at one time, he was notorious for ripping off drug dealers. I guess One-Armed Dee figured it would better to put Butchie on payroll then have him rob payroll.

Anyway, Butchie and I hit it off immediately. Anytime he'd see me on the block, he would flag me down and we would talk, laugh and joke. Butchie was a serious dude and, believe it or not, it's hard to carry that image all the time. I think when he and I would talk he would relax and turn his off "tough guy" for a few minutes. For whatever reason, we became fast friends, and I sure was glad to see him when I walked out of that cell that morning. As there usually is, there was an antagonist who, for some reason, kept stirring the pot. In K Section, it was this black dude named "Brownie" who hated me for no reason other than being white. This Brownie guy kept yelling about there's never been a white boy in K Section, which wasn't true. Others had been there and stayed, but they were white guys who were connected to drug organizations in some capacity. However, it was *unusual* for a white guy to be in Killer K. Brownie was the one who got two of the three fights started the night before because he had a big mouth and loved pumping up trouble. I wasn't going to look like a bitch after surviving three beat downs by hiding under Butchie's wing, so I said to Butchie, "Let me fight Brownie one-on-one. He's the one getting everything started, so let me and him go in a cell and duke it out."

I figured like most guys with a big mouth, he wasn't much of a threat by himself. So Butchie had big-time respect, and he let it be known I was cool. When we came back from breakfast, he made sure everybody knew who I was by saying the following: "This is my muthafuckin' homeboy, and you niggas couldn't fight him one-on-one, so check this out. Brownie, you go in the cell with him, and the one that comes out, stays." So it wasn't poetic, but it drove a few points home. Butchie knew this guy Brownie was all mouth, and true to form, he started making a big production of taking his shirt off and lacing up his sneakers, the whole time talking, talking ,talking—he was all talk and making sure the guards heard it, so ten guards came running before a punch was thrown. To be honest, I didn't want to fight. I was beat up already, and man, let me tell you, it hurts when you get hit where there's already a bruise. So I was glad he made an ass of himself. He lost points in everyone's eyes because of his transparent ruse to alert the guards. Anyway, the fight never took place, and I became the token white boy of K Section, and like I said, I wasn't the first white guy, but it was so unusual that guards walking past would stop and look at me with a quizzical look on their faces.

Thank God Butchie was there. I could have ended up dead in city jail, so if you think about it, I could have had a death sentence for a drug charge. I'm not talking about trafficking kilos or even possessing a large amount. I'm talking about enough for my own personal use. Others have died in jail and on the streets over a little bit of powder, and we shake our heads and say, "It's a damn shame" and go about our day. But it's a different story when it's someone we love. Imagine the guilt and pain that Gabe's parents feel over their son, or how about Zack's mom? Drugs already impact the family in permanent ways, but none are as permanent as death. Many things can be fixed, and families have a great way of restoring bridges others may think burned to the ground ,but death is a very real possibility for the addict—and the odds against them get worse in a prison setting. Again, addiction isn't a free pass to commit crime, but we must treat addiction as the disease it is and punish crimes for what they are.

Recidivism & Privatization

There's a reason addicts find themselves in prison again and again. I know someone is thinking "because they commit crimes," and yeah, that's the short answer, but it's also because they make it easy for some states to keep their 90% capacity rate requirement to the prison industry! I can honestly picture some of you saying the '80s catchphrase, "Whatchoo talkin' 'bout, Willis?" Well, first, I'm talkin' about how some states have deals with private prisons to keep beds filled. More and more, private prisons are popping up across the country and have been since the '80s, I'm also talking about an industry that trades on Wall Street, with shares that go up and down in direct relation to how many people they have locked up. Sounds like a plot to a seriously bad movie, and I wish that's all it was, but it's a fact of life and a direct byproduct of the War on Junkies. One of the biggest private prison owners is Corrections Corporation of America, the former Wackenhut. Strangely enough, they were founded in the early 1980's during the Reagan administration. Are you seeing a pattern here? Yes, it was Nixon who started the DEA and the War on Drugs, and make no mistake, it was Nixon who turned the addict into a criminal. He made it his duty to eradicate these morally deficient individuals (his opinion, not mine) and certainly he played his part in starting this so-called "war." If Nixon started the fire, Reagan poured gasoline on it, and then an under-informed society fanned the flames. I heard it said that the War on Drugs is unwinnable, but it's eminently fundable— meaning we're willing to spend tons of money on a task we have no hope of accomplishing! That's the American Way—if you have a problem, throw money at it till it goes away. The problem isn't a lack of money; it's the pockets that money is filling—back to private prisons.

I touched on this earlier, but I think it's worth looking at a little closer. The push for private prisons began with the Reagan administration and his inaugural speech for less government and more privatization. This was the first ingredient in a recipe for disaster. The second ingredient (from this same administration) was the harsher sentencing and get-tough-on-crime crap. These politicians spend a lot of money finding out what we want to hear—you should be seriously suspicious of someone who spends millions to get a job with a maximum expiration date of 8 years. That said, Reagan came out preaching this get-tough-on-crime and smaller government stuff, and the American people ate it up—and rightfully so. People were tired of living in war zones. However, what the big brains in Washington either forgot (and let's face it–Reagan did a lot of forgetting) or chose not to mention, was that all the laws for harsher sentencing and the get-tough-on-crime agenda is all about fixing a problem after it has occurred. Hadn't they heard that an ounce of prevention is worth a pound of cure? If you sentence someone to a hundred years, that's great. I'm sure that person won't commit more crimes in the free world, but guess what? The crime has still occurred, and when you start giving out mandatory sentences and stop judges from doing their jobs, you fill the prisons with guys who are going to be there for decades, and for those decades, the American people are footing the bill for his housing, food and healthcare.

So, what's the answer? OK, we build more prisons and open them to the private sector. Private companies get in the prison game and have to answer to whom? The Justice Department? Nope, that's for federal prisons. The commissioner of corrections? Nope. That office controls state-run prisons. Private prisons answer to shareholders, and to be brutally honest, the shareholders care about one thing—profits! Don't get me wrong. If CCA gets a contract, like the very lucrative one they have with the former Immigration and Naturalization Service (INS – now represented by three agencies within the Justice Department) they have a private company come in to audit the facility in question. So, let's look at that for just a moment. A private prison with revenue at nearly two billion, who has spent millions lobbying for tougher laws and harsher sentencing, is monitored by the private auditor hired by the very officials they have contributed heavily to, who then gives the private auditor "incentives" to audit in favor of the private prison. That seems legit, huh?

The whole thing stinks to high heaven, but hey, it's politics as usual and no one sees it. I'm not chasing ghosts here. There was a case in Pennsylvania in 2008 where a president judge and a senior judge were caught taking $2.6 million in bribes in a scheme for a private juvenile jail that is well known as the "Kids for Cash" scandal. The owner of two private prisons paid two judges to give juveniles long sentences to keep his prisons full and earn him more money. It's an outrage. .

These private prisons are big business, and the addicted are the commodity. They don't care about rehabilitation or treatment programs. If the prisons do that, the commodity won't return after release, and that hurts their profit. You can call it lobbying, incentives, contributions or any other politically correct name, but it will still be bribery at the end of the day!

How safe are these private prisons for the staff and prisoners? Not very! Let's see... you take a guy off the street who was a plumber up until last week, give him an eight-hour training course and a uniform, and then it's "OK, plumber, you're in charge of gang bangers, murderers, rapists and a lot of addicted people." I'm sure nothing could go wrong, right? Wrong. Very, very wrong. In May, 2012, a riot at CCA-operated Adams County Correctional Facility in Natchez, Mississippi, claimed the life of a corrections officer and left sixteen staff members and three prisoners injured. Twenty-five employees were held hostage during the disturbance, which was ultimately quelled by facility staff with assistance from the Mississippi Highway Patrol and the Federal Bureau of Prisons. According to a company statement, the fatality was the second time an employee had "lost his life to inmate assault." These private prisons are the new plantations, and the addicted are nothing more than slave labor. However, as long as the money continues to flow in and the politician coffers are filled with buckets and buckets of cash, it'll stay business as usual.

In Conclusion

There's a lot of information in this short book, and there's many who just can't see the forest for the trees. Young black men, Latino men and poor white men are being forced into slave labor camps, and mostly it's for the crime of being an addict with a disease they didn't ask for. The sick and suffering have no voice and feel this is what they deserve because everyone has convinced them that they are less than their fellow man. I want this to change. I want to see people treated, not locked up. I want to see our kids educated, not left to their own devices. I want everyone to have a chance at the American Dream, the human dream, because most of us, regardless of color, creed, or place of origin want the same thing: a decent job, the love and respect of our family and friends, and equality. Drug addiction is a treatable disease, but people need to demand accountability from our elected officials and independent audits of our prisons. Write your representatives and voice your concerns. Little by little, our so-called rights are dwindling, and we are becoming a policed people. Whether you believe it or not, Big Brother exists—but so do your voice and your power to change things.

I know some of you will say, "Well, this doesn't affect me. I'm not addicted, and neither are my kids." This affects all of us, and until addiction is taken out of the criminal arena and treated in the medical field, it will continue to grow. Corrections Corporation of America is just one private prison corporation, and they have revenue of nearly three billion dollars. That pays for lots of lobbying, incentives, political contributions, and even outright bribes. This attack on the sick and suffering will continue if unchecked, and if your son or daughter ends up in the crosshairs of this so-called war, you will become a casualty of the under-informed or the downright greedy. You can make a difference. Yes, YOU!

Never doubt that a small group of thoughtful, committed citizens can change the world. Indeed, it's the only thing that ever has.

—Margret Meade

I don't know if I've changed any minds, but I hope this

book really makes you research my claims. I implore you to look into it and check my facts. I'm sure you will see that there never was a War on Drugs. The drugs could have been stopped if the government wanted them stopped. No, this is clearly *The War on Junkies.*

Other Books by Freddie Jay

From the Junkie Series

The Junkie's Opinion

A Junkie's Nightmare: Coming Clean

Can be found on amazon or at
www.authorfreddiejay.com

Other writings:

Five-Minute Meditation

Can be found on Snippet app

www.ingramcontent.com/pod-product-compliance
Lightning Source LLC
Chambersburg PA
CBHW071420040426
42445CB00012BA/1224